MURDER
at
the big store

MURDER
AT
the big store

THERE'S NO STORE LIKE IT IN THE WORLD

ST. MARTIN'S PRESS • NEW YORK

For information, address St. Martin's Press, 175 Fifth Avenue, New York, N.Y. 10010.

Library of Congress Cataloging in Publication Data

Mayo, Diane.
Murder at the Big Store.
I. Title.
PS3563.A9639M84 1984 813'.54 84-17259
ISBN 0-312-55289-0 (pbk.)

First Edition
10 9 8 7 6 5 4 3 2 1

FOR SUSANNAH, MARY ANNE, AND BRUCE

I would like to thank the Edward Albee Foundation; also Leslie Pockell, Tom Dunne, Edward Albee, Steve Latham, and Amy Turner.

All the characters in this book, including the store, are fictional.

MURDER

at

the big store

THE BIG STORE HAD JUST OPENED WHEN A. TUNA ARRIVED.

THE BIG S
WHY DOESN'T MY MOTHER EVER GIVE ME A PRESENT I CAN USE?
THEY'RE HAVING A SABLE COAT SALE TODAY
YOU CAN NEVER HAVE TOO MANY
THE REVEREND MOON WANTS YOU TO HAVE THIS FLOWER— TWO-FIFTY
BEAT IT, YOU LITTLE RAT
YAY

Renfield, the zoophagous window trimmer, had worked all night to finish the displays for the store's newest promotion, "explore the arctic!!" He had done a brilliant job of transforming the giant windows into a frozen wasteland. Two world-famous designers, Rolf L'Orange and Ikō, had been invited to appear at the big store that day. Renfield hated having designers in the store.

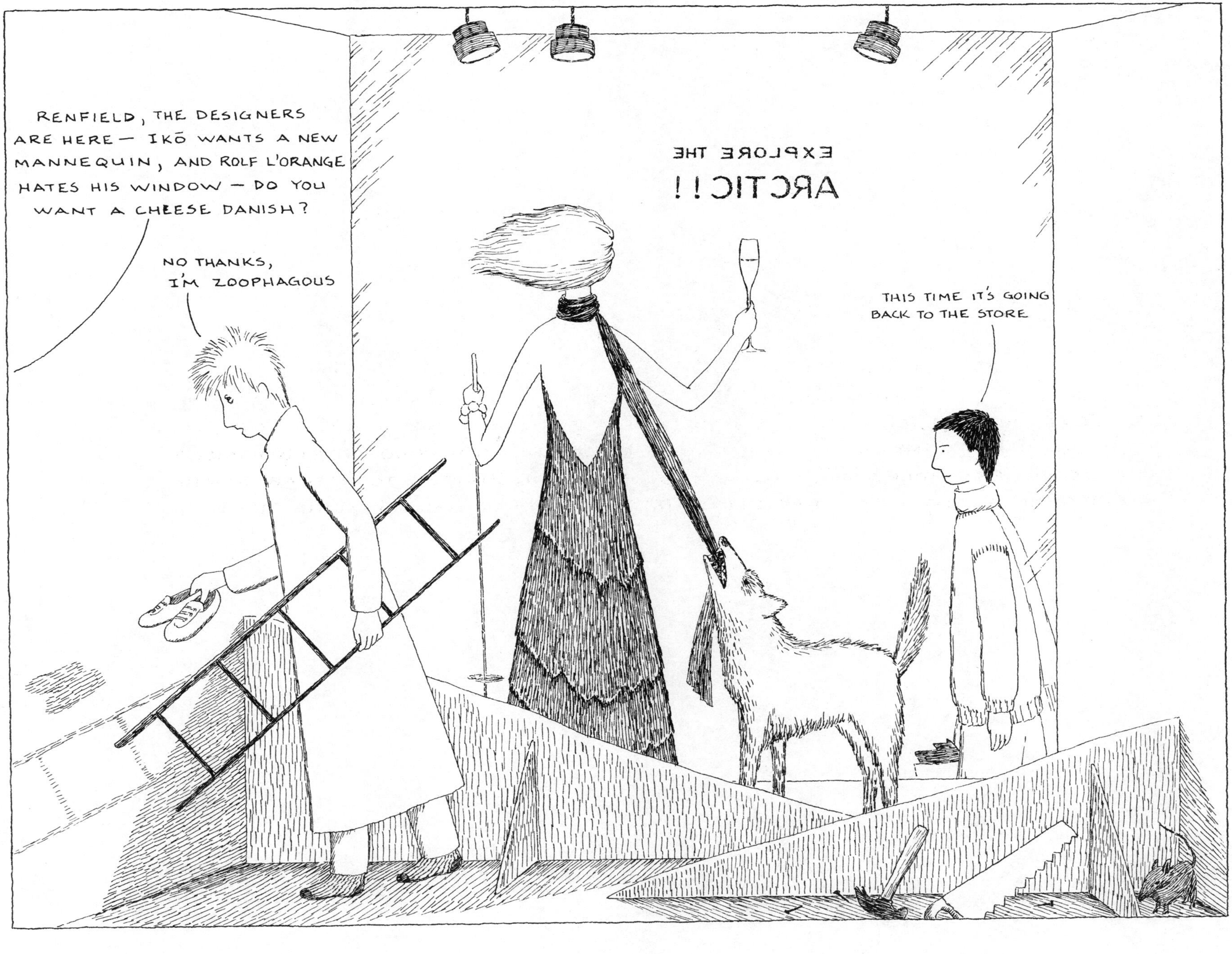
RENFIELD, THE DESIGNERS ARE HERE— IKŌ WANTS A NEW MANNEQUIN, AND ROLF L'ORANGE HATES HIS WINDOW — DO YOU WANT A CHEESE DANISH?
NO THANKS, I'M ZOOPHAGOUS
EXPLORE THE ARCTIC!!
THIS TIME IT'S GOING BACK TO THE STORE

ROLF L'ORANGE HAD REACHED THE TOP OF HIS PROFESSION, BUT HE WAS NOT HAPPY.

Rolf L'Orange
Americana
MIRROR, MIRROR ON THE WALL, WHO'S THE MOST FAMOUS DESIGNER OF ALL
IT'S IKŌ
WHO SAID THAT?
I WANT TO RETURN A TELEPHONE
WELL, I'M CERTAINLY NOT GOING TO HELP YOU
CUSTOMER ASSISTANCE
meet Rolf L'Orange today on 5 at 4

IKŌ AND ROLF L'ORANGE HAD MET BEFORE, WHEN IKŌ WON THE PRESTIGIOUS GATSBY AWARD. AT THE DINNER WHICH FOLLOWED THE PRESENTATION SHE HAD SPILLED CREAM OF MUSSEL SOUP ON HIS FAVORITE SILVER-TOED COWBOY BOOTS. HE HAD MANAGED TO POUR MOST OF HIS AFTER DINNER COFFEE DOWN THE BACK OF HER DRESS, BUT HIS BOOTS WERE RUINED.

人よりもかゝしの多き在所かな
TOO BAD, ROLF–
THOUGHT YOU HAD
IT SEWN UP... HEH, HEH
BORING
SPEECH
OH
GO AHEAD AND LAUGH,
ALVIN – YOU DIDN'T
WIN EITHER
SHE LOOKS LIKE A
PILE OF OLD NEWSPAPERS

THE CONVERSATION BETWEEN THE TWO DESIGNERS WAS BECOMING STRAINED WHEN MAX CAME TO GREET THEM. MAX HAD BEEN A SUPERVISOR AT THE BIG STORE FOR FIFTEEN YEARS. HE WANTED TO BE AN EXECUTIVE, BUT HE HAD NEVER BEEN PROMOTED BECAUSE HE ALWAYS WORE THE WRONG TIE.

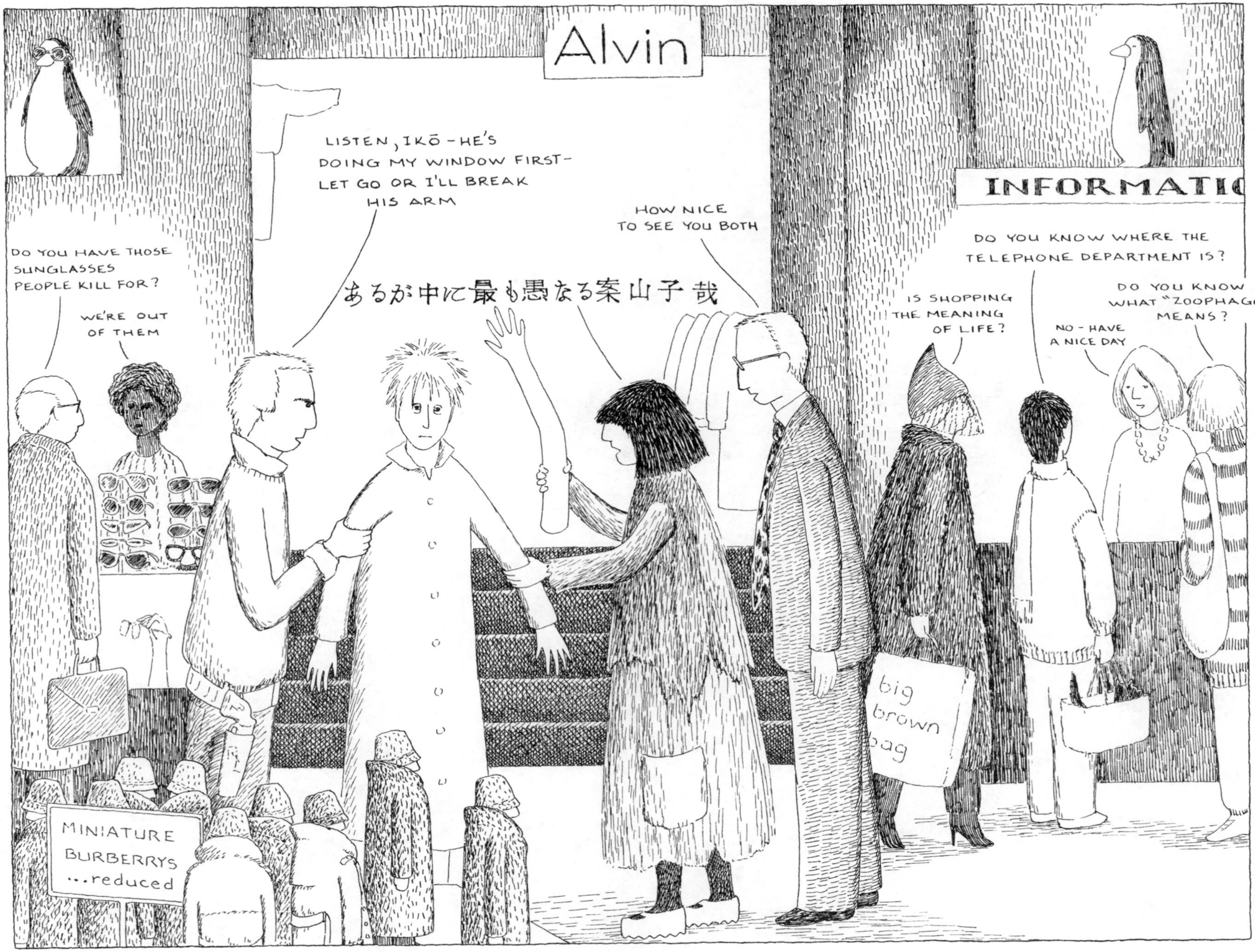

Alvin
INFORMATIC
LISTEN, IKŌ-HE'S DOING MY WINDOW FIRST- LET GO OR I'LL BREAK HIS ARM
あるが中に最も愚なる案山子哉
HOW NICE TO SEE YOU BOTH
DO YOU HAVE THOSE SUNGLASSES PEOPLE KILL FOR?
WE'RE OUT OF THEM
DO YOU KNOW WHERE THE TELEPHONE DEPARTMENT IS?
IS SHOPPING THE MEANING OF LIFE?
NO - HAVE A NICE DAY
DO YOU KNOW WHAT "ZOOPHAGOUS" MEANS?
big brown bag
MINIATURE BURBERRYS ...reduced

ONE OF THE STORE'S MANY VICE-PRESIDENTS HAD RECENTLY BEEN ASPHYXIATED, AND MAX WAS WAITING FOR AN OPPORTUNE MOMENT TO ASK THE DESIGNERS' ADVICE ABOUT TIES.

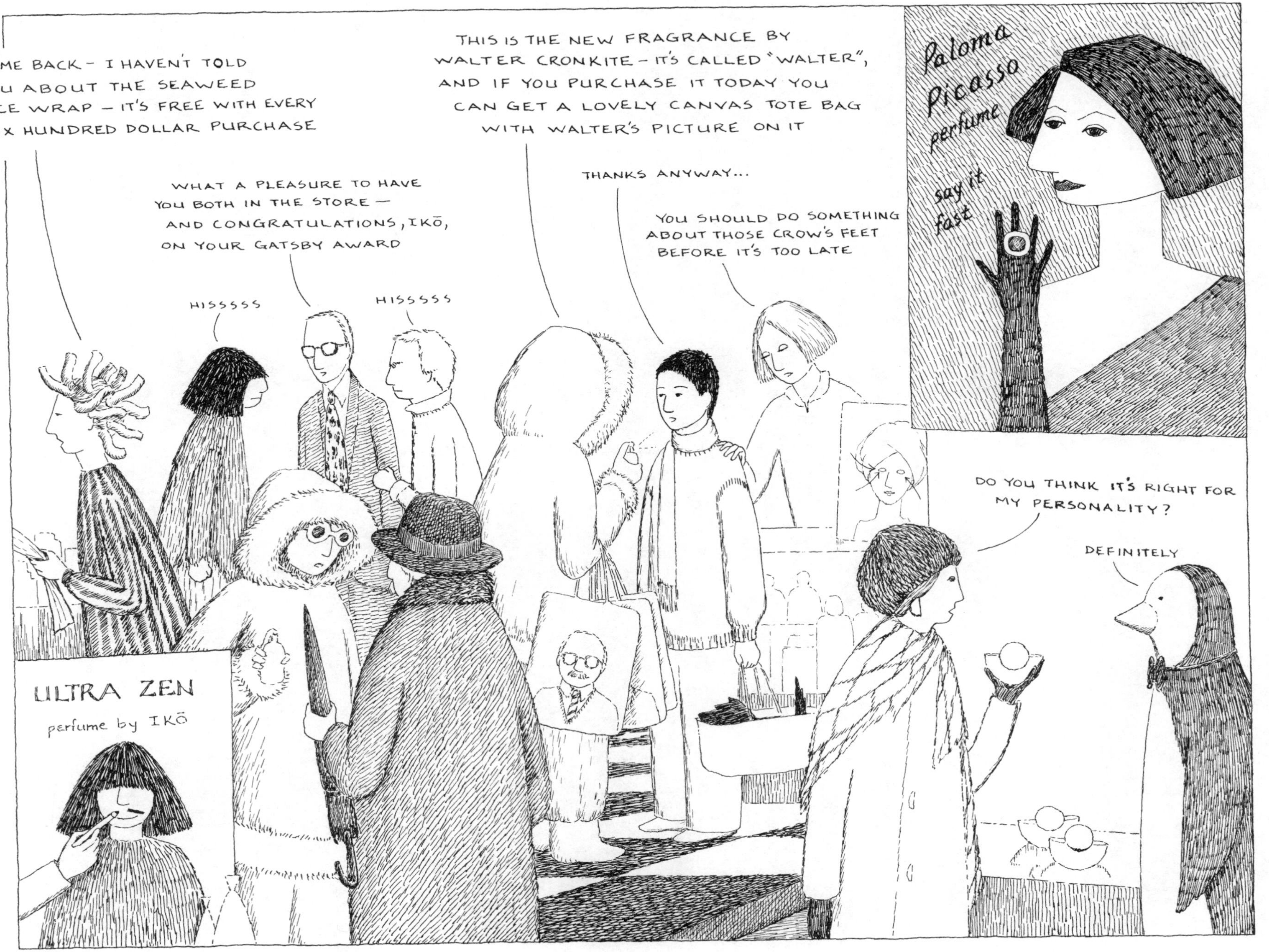
COME BACK – I HAVEN'T TOLD YOU ABOUT THE SEAWEED FACE WRAP – IT'S FREE WITH EVERY SIX HUNDRED DOLLAR PURCHASE
HISSSSS
WHAT A PLEASURE TO HAVE YOU BOTH IN THE STORE – AND CONGRATULATIONS, IKŌ, ON YOUR GATSBY AWARD
HISSSSS
THIS IS THE NEW FRAGRANCE BY WALTER CRONKITE – IT'S CALLED "WALTER", AND IF YOU PURCHASE IT TODAY YOU CAN GET A LOVELY CANVAS TOTE BAG WITH WALTER'S PICTURE ON IT
THANKS ANYWAY...
YOU SHOULD DO SOMETHING ABOUT THOSE CROW'S FEET BEFORE IT'S TOO LATE
Paloma Picasso perfume
say it fast
DO YOU THINK IT'S RIGHT FOR MY PERSONALITY?
DEFINITELY
ULTRA ZEN
perfume by IKŌ

A. TUNA DECIDED TO TRY ANOTHER FLOOR. NEAR THE ELEVATOR SHE NOTICED A LARGE BROWN BEAR. MARTY, THE STORE DETECTIVE, ALWAYS DISGUISED HIMSELF TO MATCH THE THEME OF THE STORE. HE HAD LEARNED THIS TECHNIQUE FROM A BOOK CALLED "HOW TO BE A DEPARTMENT STORE DETECTIVE", WHICH HE KEPT IN HIS POCKET FOR EMERGENCIES.

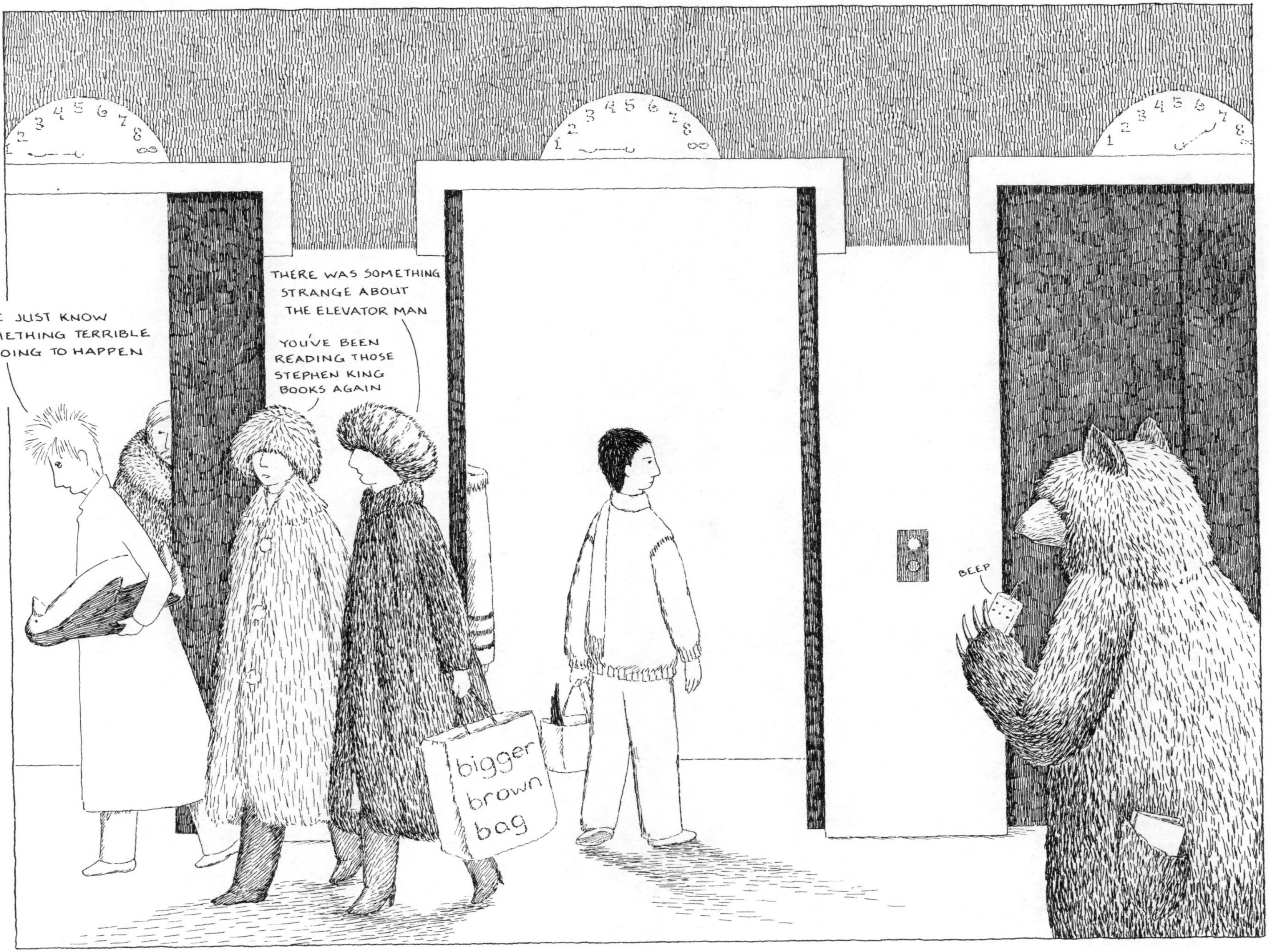
I JUST KNOW SOMETHING TERRIBLE IS GOING TO HAPPEN
THERE WAS SOMETHING STRANGE ABOUT THE ELEVATOR MAN
YOU'VE BEEN READING THOSE STEPHEN KING BOOKS AGAIN
bigger brown bag
BEEP

THE ELEVATOR MAN WAS DEAD.

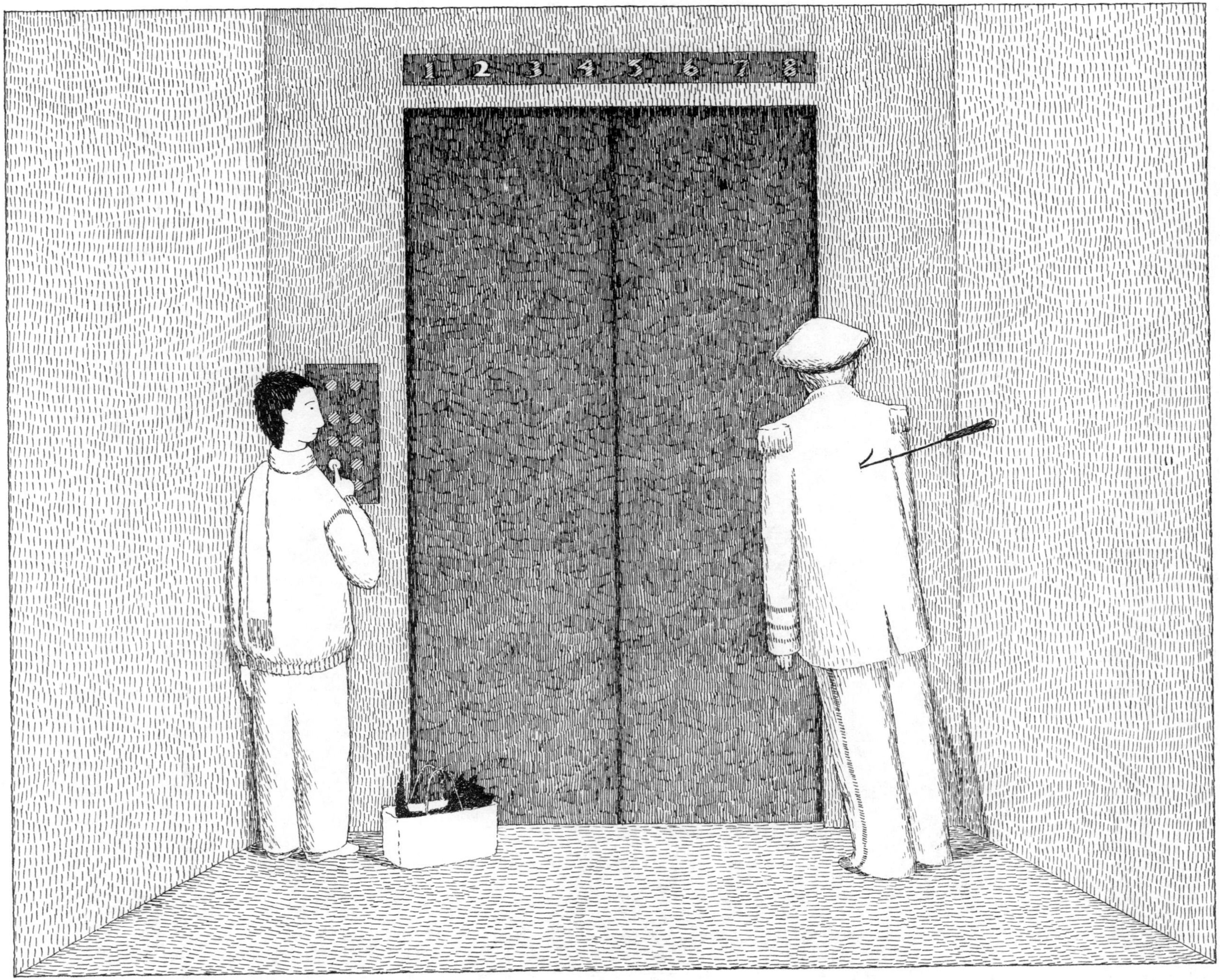
1 2 3 4 5 6 7 8

WAS HE MURDERED?

WHAT WAS ROLF L'ORANGE WEARING AT THE GATSBY AWARDS?

DOES MAX UNDERSTAND JAPANESE?

WHY DOESN'T RENFIELD CAST A SHADOW?

WHAT IS THE STORE DETECTIVE'S NAME?

WHAT IS THE WORST EXPERIENCE YOU HAVE EVER HAD IN A DEPARTMENT STORE?

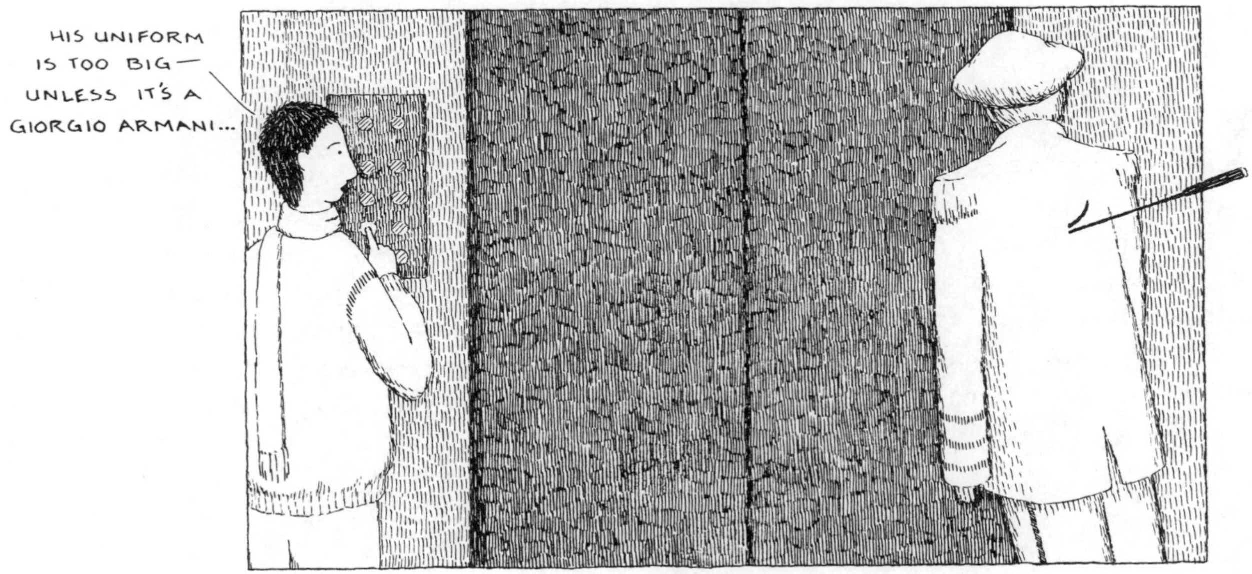
HIS UNIFORM IS TOO BIG— UNLESS IT'S A GIORGIO ARMANI...

IKŌ HAD TAKEN OVER MOST OF THE SECOND FLOOR. EVERYONE WANTED HER CLOTHES. A RECENT ISSUE OF VOGUE HAD BEEN DEVOTED ENTIRELY TO IKŌ; THE COVER STORY WAS TITLED "THROW OUT THOSE BORING CLASSICS, IKŌ IS HERE!" A WELL KNOWN PUBLISHER WANTED TO DO HER LIFE STORY AND IT WAS RUMORED THAT SHE WAS ABOUT TO INTRODUCE HER FIRST COLLECTION OF HOME FURNISHINGS, CALLED "PAPER HOUSE." IT SEEMED THAT THERE WAS NO STOPPING HER.

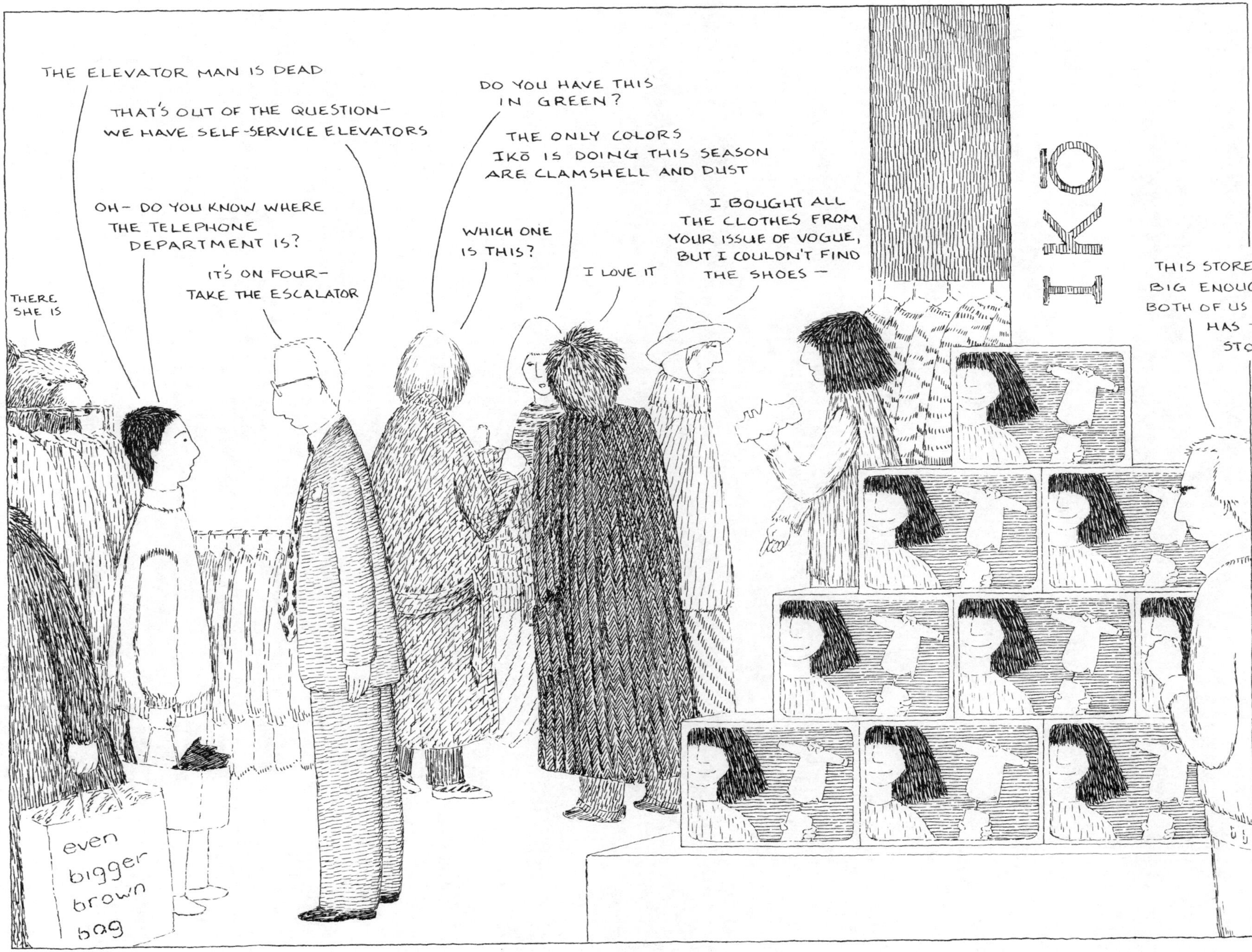
THE ELEVATOR MAN IS DEAD
THAT'S OUT OF THE QUESTION– WE HAVE SELF-SERVICE ELEVATORS
DO YOU HAVE THIS IN GREEN?
THE ONLY COLORS IKŌ IS DOING THIS SEASON ARE CLAMSHELL AND DUST
OH– DO YOU KNOW WHERE THE TELEPHONE DEPARTMENT IS?
IT'S ON FOUR– TAKE THE ESCALATOR
WHICH ONE IS THIS?
I LOVE IT
I BOUGHT ALL THE CLOTHES FROM YOUR ISSUE OF VOGUE, BUT I COULDN'T FIND THE SHOES –
THERE SHE IS
IKŌ
THIS STORE ISN'T BIG ENOUGH FOR BOTH OF US – SHE HAS TO BE STOPPED
even bigger brown bag

FOLLOWING MAX'S DIRECTIONS, A. TUNA FOUND THE TELEPHONE DEPARTMENT, WHERE A BUSY CLERK EXPLAINED THE REFUND PROCEDURE.

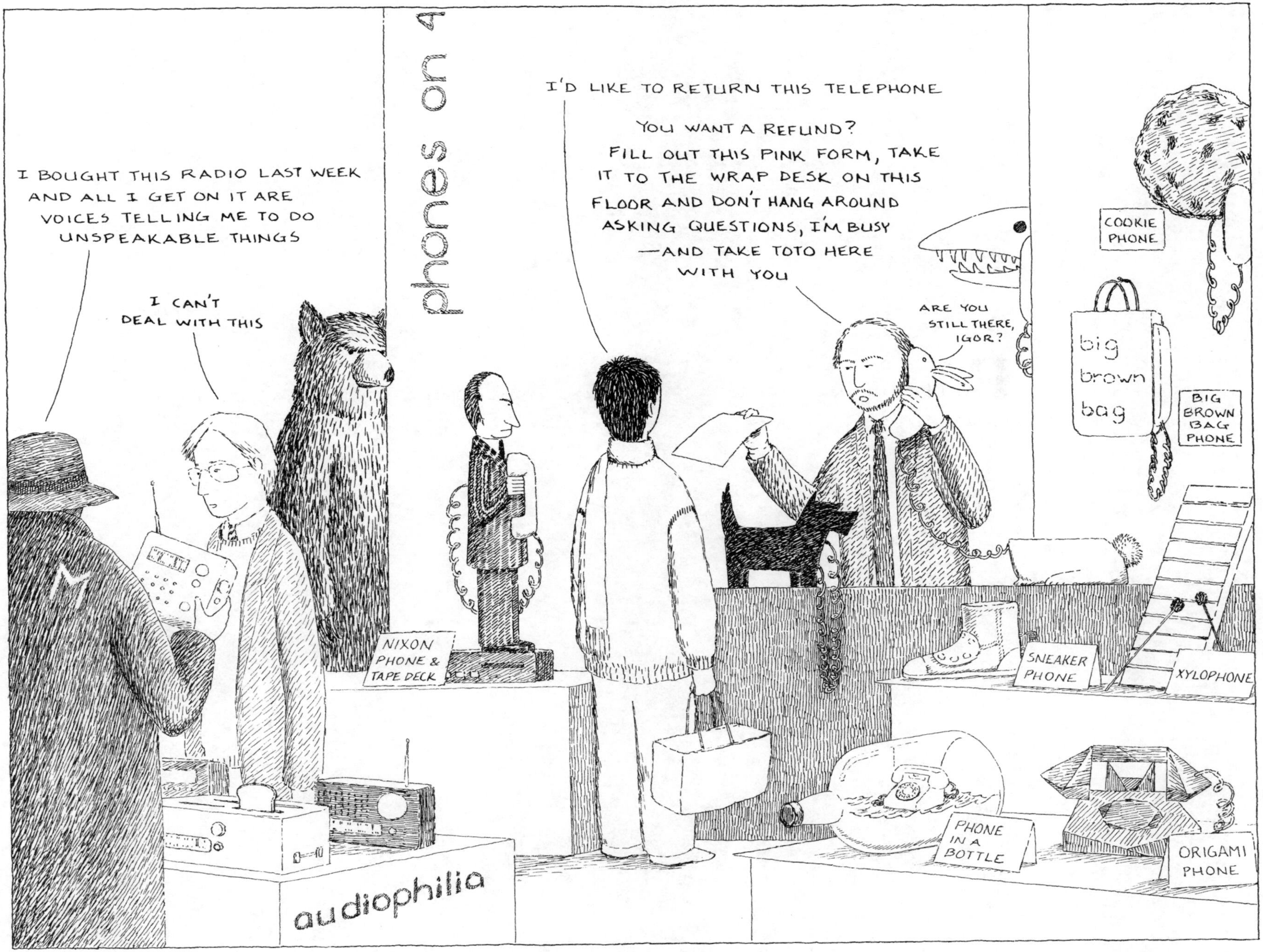

I BOUGHT THIS RADIO LAST WEEK AND ALL I GET ON IT ARE VOICES TELLING ME TO DO UNSPEAKABLE THINGS
I CAN'T DEAL WITH THIS
phones on 4
I'D LIKE TO RETURN THIS TELEPHONE
YOU WANT A REFUND? FILL OUT THIS PINK FORM, TAKE IT TO THE WRAP DESK ON THIS FLOOR AND DON'T HANG AROUND ASKING QUESTIONS, I'M BUSY —AND TAKE TOTO HERE WITH YOU
ARE YOU STILL THERE, IGOR?
COOKIE PHONE
big brown bag
BIG BROWN BAG PHONE
NIXON PHONE & TAPE DECK
SNEAKER PHONE
XYLOPHONE
PHONE IN A BOTTLE
ORIGAMI PHONE
audiophilia

REFUNDS AND GIFT WRAPPING WERE BOTH DONE AT THE WRAP DESK.

THERE WAS ALWAYS A WAITING LINE.

I CAN ALMOST SEE THE WRAP DESK
I'VE FORGOTTEN WHETHER I'M BUYING THESE CLOTHES OR BRINGING THEM BACK
WHAT DID YOU BUY?
THREE DOZEN WINEGLASSES— I'M HAVING EACH ONE WRAPPED INDIVIDUALLY
NOT ANY MORE
I'VE BEEN HERE FOR TWO HOURS
I'VE BEEN HERE FOR TWO DAYS
I LIVE HERE— I'M A VICTIM OF GENTRIFICATION
HERE'S MY CARD— I'M A TENANT LAWYER
WHAT IS THAT THING YOU'RE POKING ME WITH AND HOW DO YOU EXPECT TO HAVE IT WRAPPED?
IT'S A FLAGPOLE
POST
"RADIO KILLER" STRIKES AGAIN!
SMASH
GLASS
FRAGIL

I'M RETURNING ALL THE ROLF L'ORANGE THINGS I BOUGHT LAST WEEK— VOGUE SAYS CLASSICS ARE BORING
I KNOW—I'M BRINGING BACK ALL MY ALVINS EXCEPT THE UNDERWEAR
THIS REMINDS ME OF A MOVIE I SAW ON T.V. LAST NIGHT— IT WAS "THE ISLAND OF DR. MOREAU", THE ORIGINAL VERSION WITH BELA LUGOSI....
TELL ME ABOUT IT
SHHH—I'M LISTENING TO THIS
I DON'T THINK THIS LINE IS MOVING AT ALL— DO YOU THINK IT'S MOVING?
NO—NOT THAT— I WON'T DO THAT
THEY'LL NEVER FIND ME HERE
A VAMPIRE?
EXCUSE ME—YOU LOOK AS IF YOU WORK HERE— I'VE FILLED OUT THIS PINK REFUND FORM BUT I'M NOT SURE ABOUT THE LAST QUESTION, "ARE YOU NOW OR HAVE YOU EVER BEEN...
CHAPTER SIX— SHADOWING THE SUSPECT
monster brown bag

RENFIELD SEEMED INTERESTED IN A.TUNA'S PROBLEM. HE WAS FAMILIAR WITH THE STORE'S COMPLICATED REFUND SYSTEM, SO HE WAS ABLE TO GIVE HER SOME USEFUL ADVICE.

I HOPE THEY HAVE A BOX FOR IT
THE BEST UNDERWEAR COMES FROM A LITTLE SHOP IN MILAN
I KNOW, I'VE BEEN THERE
. . . AND RAYMOND BURR HAD TURNED ALL THESE PEOPLE INTO ANIMALS, AND HE KEPT THEM CHAINED UP IN A PIT, BUT THEY WERE STILL HALF HUMAN...
NO, HE TURNED ANIMALS INTO PEOPLE- I'VE SEEN IT
I HAVEN'T SEEN IT- I WANT TO KNOW WHAT HAPPENS NEXT
THIS LINE ISN'T MOVING
YOU WANT ME TO DO THAT AGAIN? I CAN'T- I WON'T- I MIGHT...
THIS PINK FORM IS NO GOOD WITHOUT A GREEN FORM- THEY SHOULD HAVE SENT YOU TO THE LAMP DEPARTMENT FOR THAT- BY THE WAY, I'M RENFIELD- IF I WERE YOU, I'D LEAVE THE STORE- I JUST KNOW SOMETHING TERRIBLE IS GOING TO HAPPEN
THERE ISN'T ANY ELEVATOR MAN
DO YOU KNOW ABOUT THE ELEVATOR MAN?
MAINTAIN A LOW PROFILE
monster brown bag

In the lamp department, A. Tuna began to suspect that she was being followed.

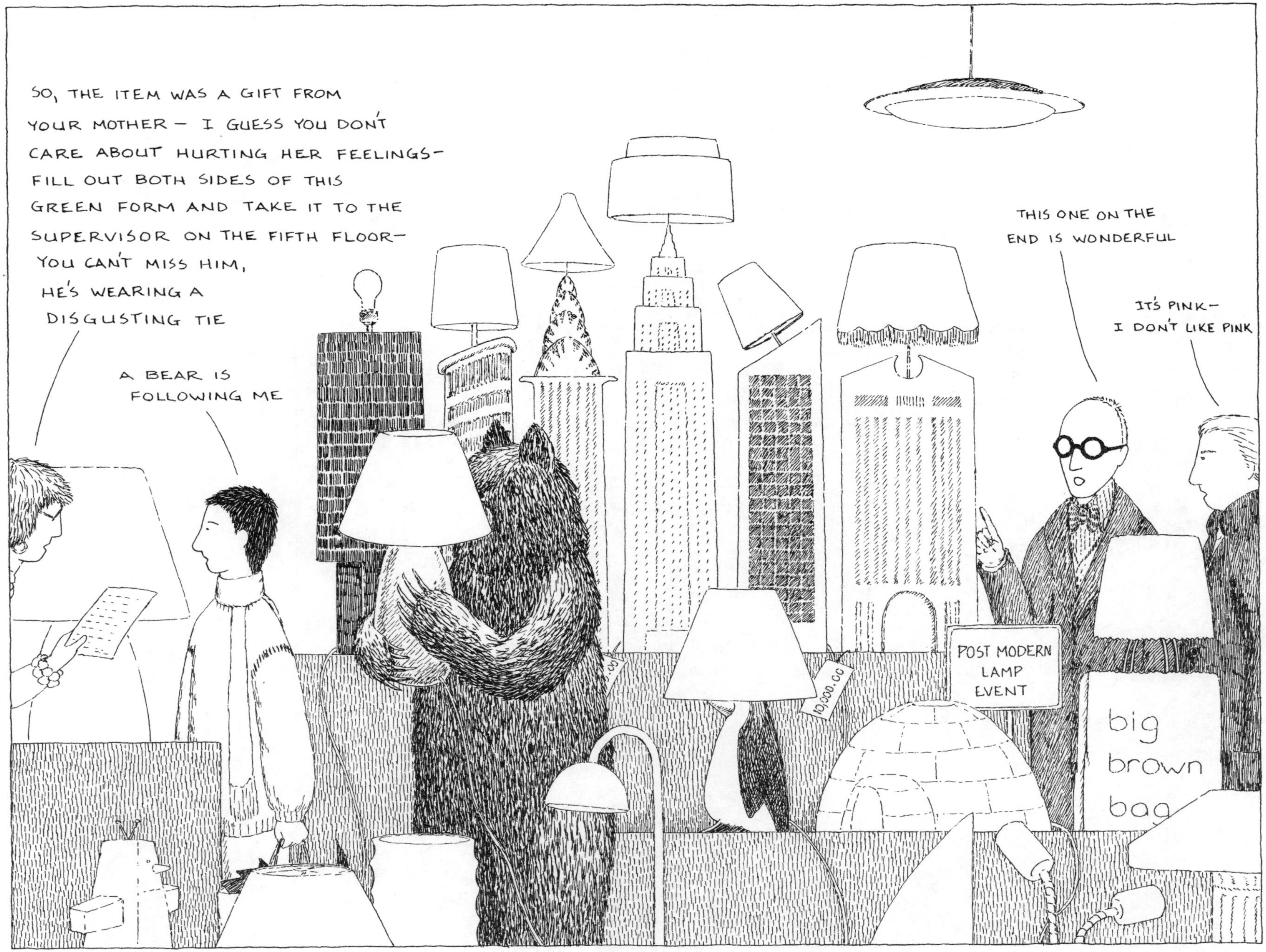
SO, THE ITEM WAS A GIFT FROM YOUR MOTHER — I GUESS YOU DON'T CARE ABOUT HURTING HER FEELINGS— FILL OUT BOTH SIDES OF THIS GREEN FORM AND TAKE IT TO THE SUPERVISOR ON THE FIFTH FLOOR— YOU CAN'T MISS HIM, HE'S WEARING A DISGUSTING TIE
A BEAR IS FOLLOWING ME
THIS ONE ON THE END IS WONDERFUL
IT'S PINK— I DON'T LIKE PINK
POST MODERN LAMP EVENT
10,000.00
big brown bag

What bear?

HOW DID A. TUNA GET TO THE FOURTH FLOOR?

WHAT WAS RENFIELD DOING IN THE WRAP
DESK LINE?

DOES THE BEST UNDERWEAR REALLY COME
FROM MILAN?

WHAT WAS JAY GATSBY'S REAL NAME?

WHAT TIME IS IT?

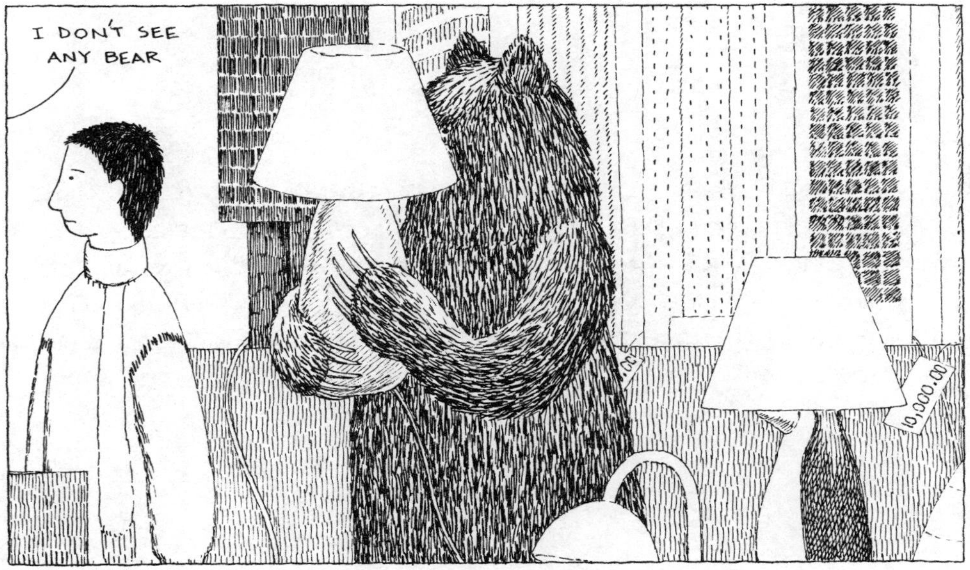
I DON'T SEE ANY BEAR
10,000.00

THE MODEL ROOMS ON THE FIFTH FLOOR WERE ONE OF THE STORE'S BIGGEST ATTRACTIONS. THEY HAD JUST BEEN DECORATED FOR "EXPLORE THE ARCTIC!!"; RENFIELD HAD SPENT HOURS PAINTING EACH SNOWFLAKE ON THE FALSE WINDOWS. ROLF L'ORANGE HAD CREATED A STRIKINGLY BEAUTIFUL ROOM WHICH HAD ALREADY BEEN PHOTOGRAPHED FOR A SPECIAL ISSUE OF "UPSCALE HOME", STILL HE WAS NOT HAPPY.

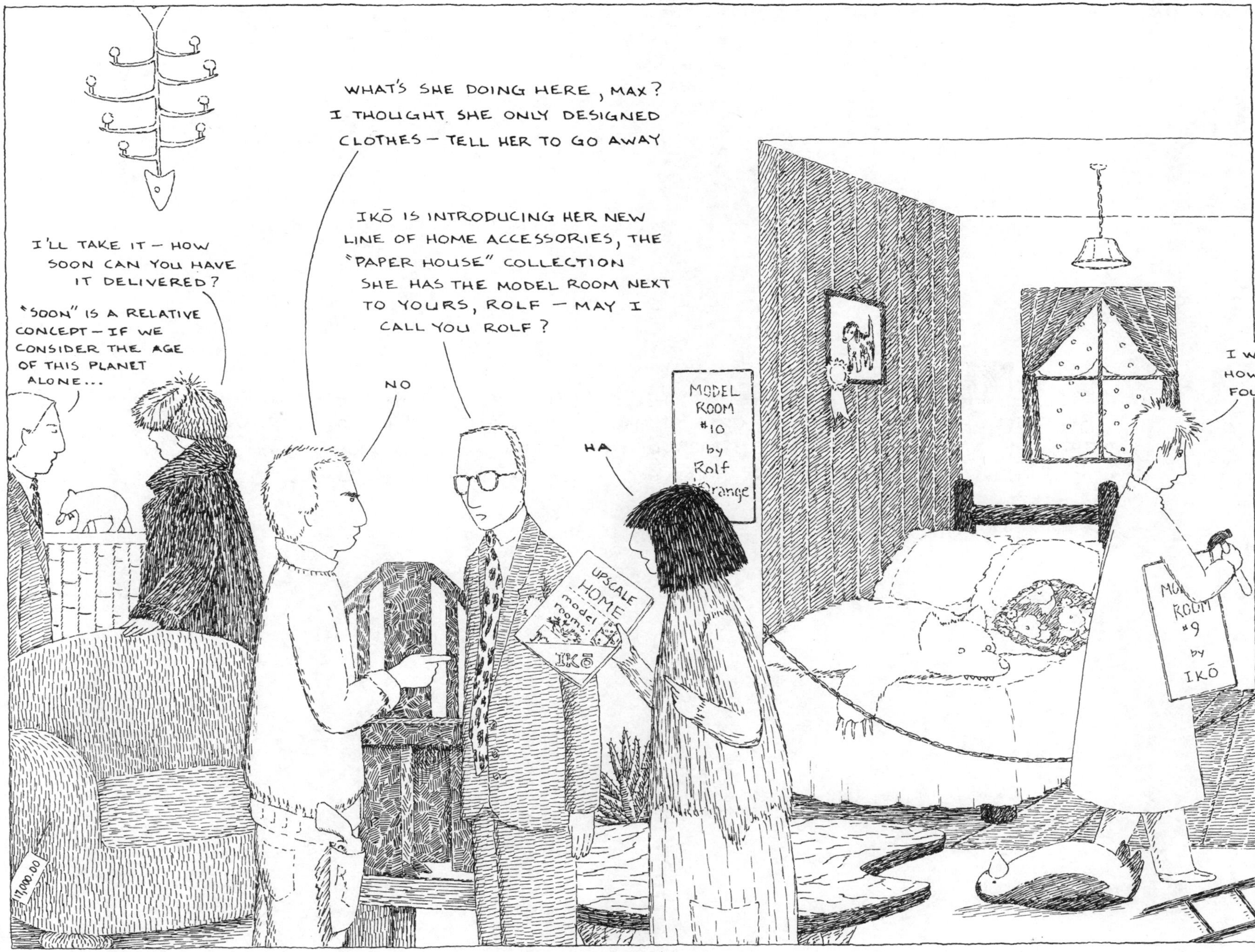
I'LL TAKE IT — HOW SOON CAN YOU HAVE IT DELIVERED?
"SOON" IS A RELATIVE CONCEPT — IF WE CONSIDER THE AGE OF THIS PLANET ALONE...
WHAT'S SHE DOING HERE, MAX? I THOUGHT SHE ONLY DESIGNED CLOTHES — TELL HER TO GO AWAY
IKŌ IS INTRODUCING HER NEW LINE OF HOME ACCESSORIES, THE "PAPER HOUSE" COLLECTION
SHE HAS THE MODEL ROOM NEXT TO YOURS, ROLF — MAY I CALL YOU ROLF?
NO
HA
UPSCALE HOME model rooms
IKŌ
MODEL ROOM #10 by Rolf
I WONDER HOW THEY FOUND ME
ROOM #9 by IKŌ
17,000.00

MAX'S DESK WAS IN A DUSTY CORNER OF THE FIFTH FLOOR FURNITURE DEPARTMENT. HE OFTEN THOUGHT OF THE LUXURIOUS PRIVATE OFFICE ON THE EIGHTH FLOOR THAT WOULD BE HIS WHEN HIS PROMOTION CAME. HE WAS THINKING ABOUT CARPET SWATCHES WHEN HE NOTICED A. TUNA.

IT'S YOU AGAIN – HAVE YOU SEEN ANY MORE IMAGINARY ELEVATOR MEN? WHAT IS THAT REPULSIVE OBJECT ON MY DESK?
IT'S A TELEPHONE THAT BARKS – YOU CAN SEE WHY I WANT TO RETURN IT –
NO, IT'S CHARMING
A BEAR IS FOLLOWING ME
BY THE WAY, MAX, YOU DIDN'T GET THAT PROMOTION – IT'S YOUR TIE
"PAPER HOUSE"... SHE COULDN'T DESIGN HER WAY OUT OF A PAPER BAG
SOLD
MAX
SUPERVISOR
UPSCALE HOME
MODEL ROOMS
IKŌ
NEW COLORS
CLAMSHELL DUST

A. TUNA WAS NOT SURPRISED WHEN MAX GAVE HER ANOTHER FORM TO FILL OUT. THIS ONE WAS BEIGE, AND IT WAS TWO PAGES LONG.

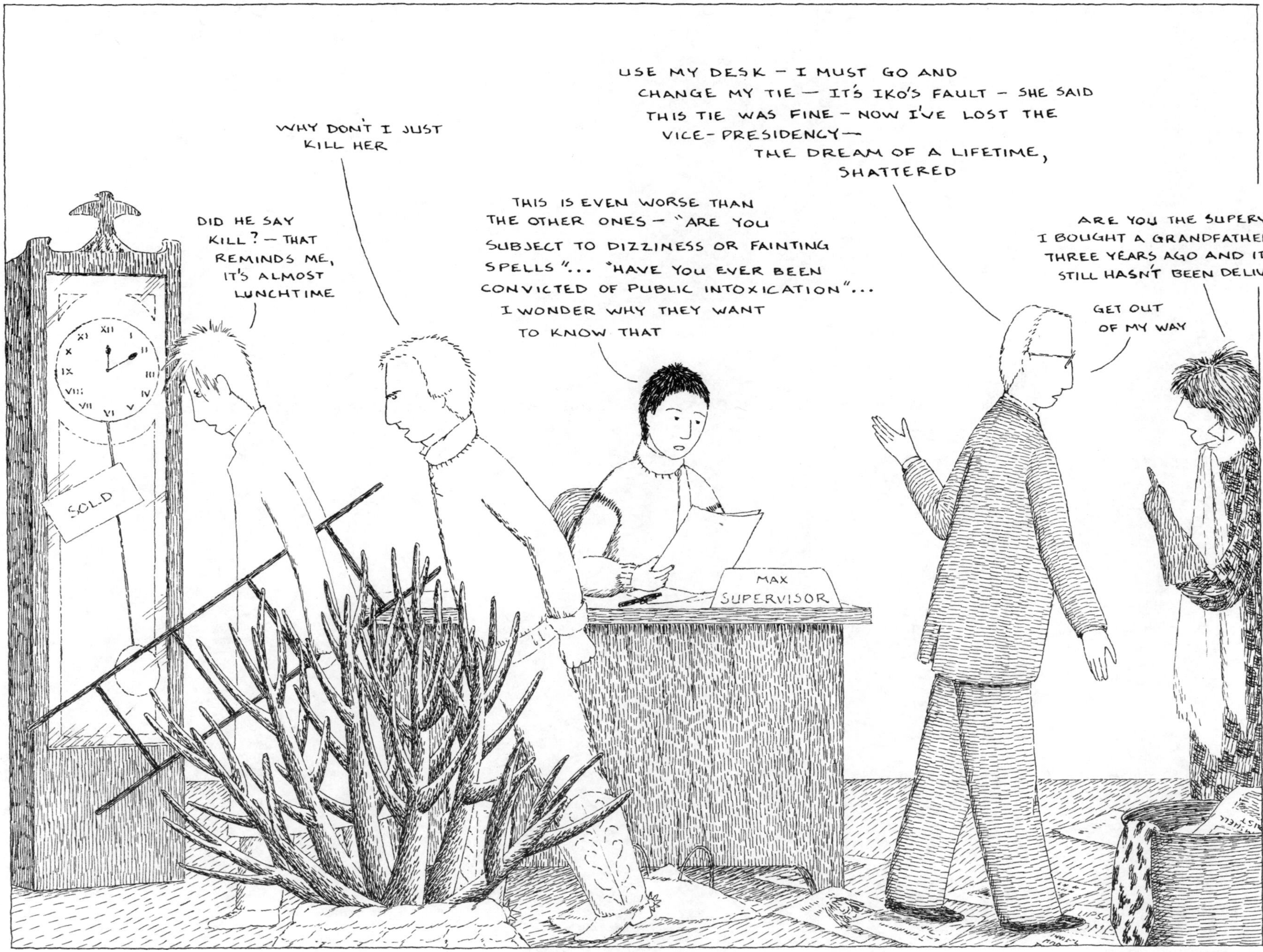
DID HE SAY KILL? — THAT REMINDS ME, IT'S ALMOST LUNCHTIME
WHY DON'T I JUST KILL HER
THIS IS EVEN WORSE THAN THE OTHER ONES — "ARE YOU SUBJECT TO DIZZINESS OR FAINTING SPELLS"... "HAVE YOU EVER BEEN CONVICTED OF PUBLIC INTOXICATION"... I WONDER WHY THEY WANT TO KNOW THAT
USE MY DESK — I MUST GO AND CHANGE MY TIE — IT'S IKO'S FAULT — SHE SAID THIS TIE WAS FINE — NOW I'VE LOST THE VICE-PRESIDENCY — THE DREAM OF A LIFETIME, SHATTERED
GET OUT OF MY WAY
ARE YOU THE SUPERVISOR? I BOUGHT A GRANDFATHER CLOCK THREE YEARS AGO AND IT STILL HASN'T BEEN DELIVERED
SOLD
MAX
SUPERVISOR

SHE HAD JUST FINISHED THE SECOND PAGE WHEN MAX RETURNED.

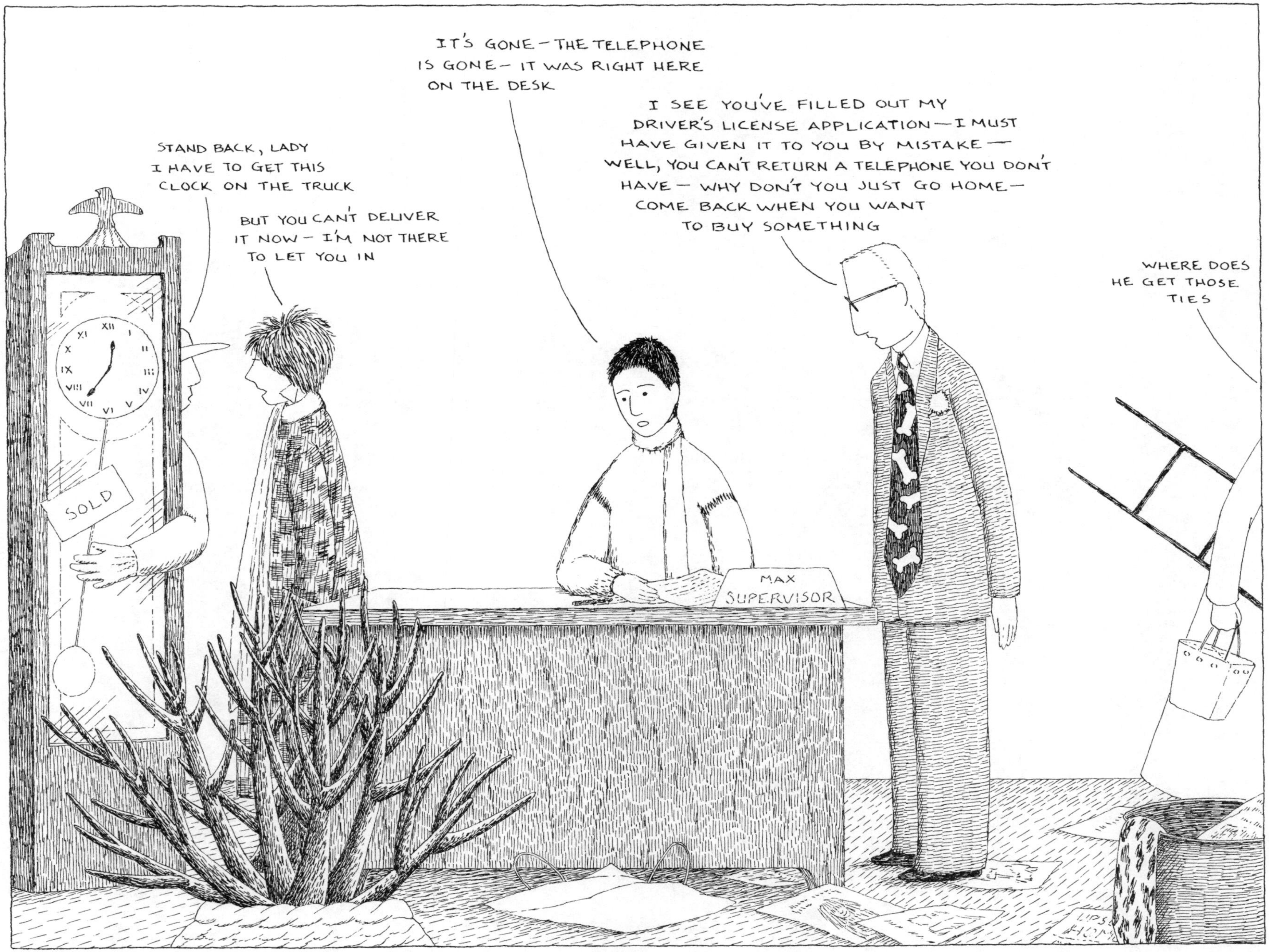
STAND BACK, LADY I HAVE TO GET THIS CLOCK ON THE TRUCK
BUT YOU CAN'T DELIVER IT NOW — I'M NOT THERE TO LET YOU IN
IT'S GONE — THE TELEPHONE IS GONE — IT WAS RIGHT HERE ON THE DESK
I SEE YOU'VE FILLED OUT MY DRIVER'S LICENSE APPLICATION — I MUST HAVE GIVEN IT TO YOU BY MISTAKE — WELL, YOU CAN'T RETURN A TELEPHONE YOU DON'T HAVE — WHY DON'T YOU JUST GO HOME — COME BACK WHEN YOU WANT TO BUY SOMETHING
WHERE DOES HE GET THOSE TIES
SOLD
MAX SUPERVISOR

A. TUNA DECIDED TO TAKE MAX'S ADVICE AND JUST GO HOME. THE TELEPHONE HAD BEEN HEAVIER THAN IT LOOKED AND SHE WAS GLAD TO BE RID OF IT, EVEN WITHOUT A REFUND. SHE WAS LOOKING FOR THE ESCALATOR WHEN A SOUND COMING FROM ONE OF THE MODEL ROOMS MADE HER PAUSE. SHE HAD HEARD THAT SOUND BEFORE.

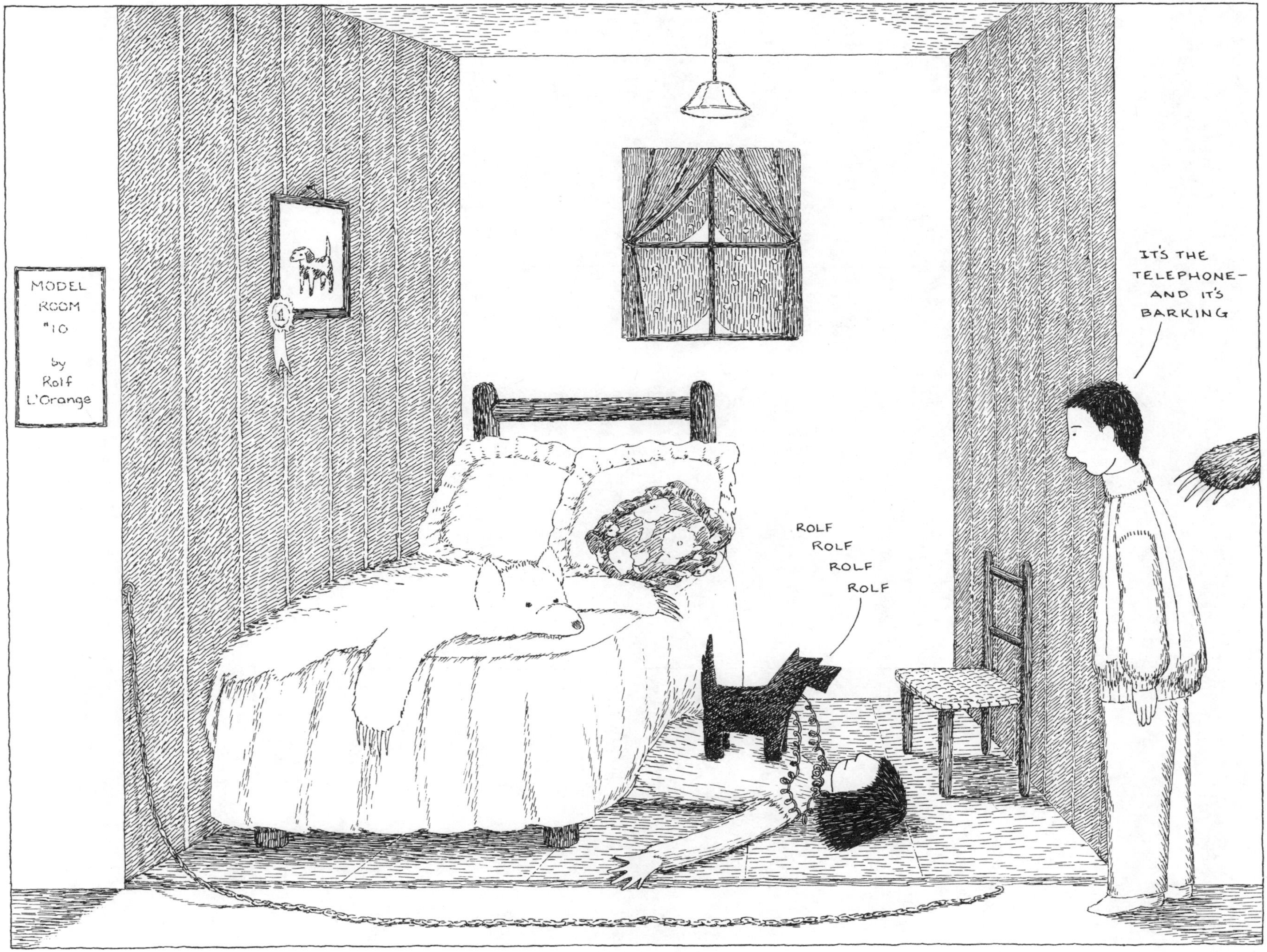
MODEL ROOM #10 by Rolf L'Orange
IT'S THE TELEPHONE— AND IT'S BARKING
ROLF ROLF ROLF ROLF

WHO KILLED IKO?

    YOU NOW HAVE ALL THE CLUES THAT ARE NECESSARY TO SOLVE THE MURDER OF IKŌ.

    ZOOPHAGOUS MEANS "LIFE-EATING."

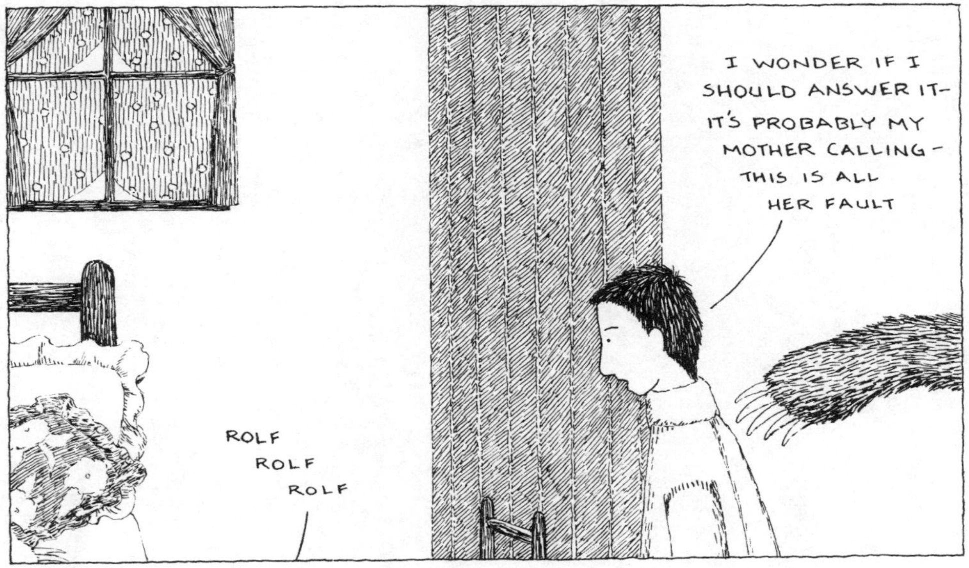
ROLF
ROLF
ROLF
I WONDER IF I SHOULD ANSWER IT— IT'S PROBABLY MY MOTHER CALLING— THIS IS ALL HER FAULT

THE TELEPHONE STOPPED BARKING. IKŌ HAD BEEN STRANGLED. IT WAS LUNCHTIME.

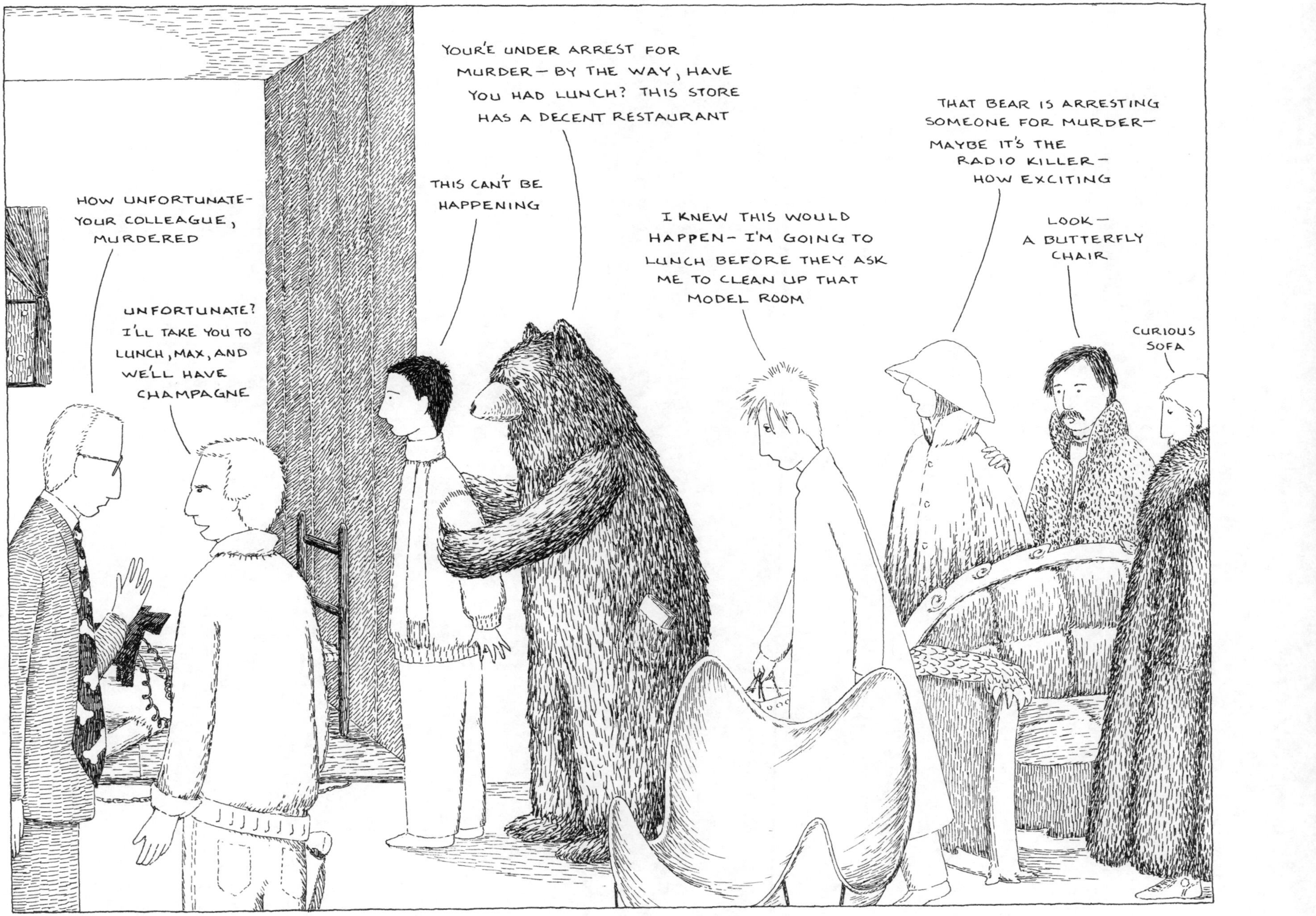
HOW UNFORTUNATE- YOUR COLLEAGUE, MURDERED
UNFORTUNATE? I'LL TAKE YOU TO LUNCH, MAX, AND WE'LL HAVE CHAMPAGNE
THIS CAN'T BE HAPPENING
YOUR'E UNDER ARREST FOR MURDER— BY THE WAY, HAVE YOU HAD LUNCH? THIS STORE HAS A DECENT RESTAURANT
I KNEW THIS WOULD HAPPEN— I'M GOING TO LUNCH BEFORE THEY ASK ME TO CLEAN UP THAT MODEL ROOM
THAT BEAR IS ARRESTING SOMEONE FOR MURDER— MAYBE IT'S THE RADIO KILLER— HOW EXCITING
LOOK— A BUTTERFLY CHAIR
CURIOUS SOFA

JUMP! WAS THE BEST RESTAURANT IN THE STORE. IT HAD BEEN NAMED
AFTER ITS CHEF, THE FAMOUS MARLON JUMP FROM CALIFORNIA, WHO DID
ALL THE COOKING ON A HIGH PLATFORM IN THE CENTER OF THE DINING ROOM.
THE FOOD WAS EXCEPTIONAL.

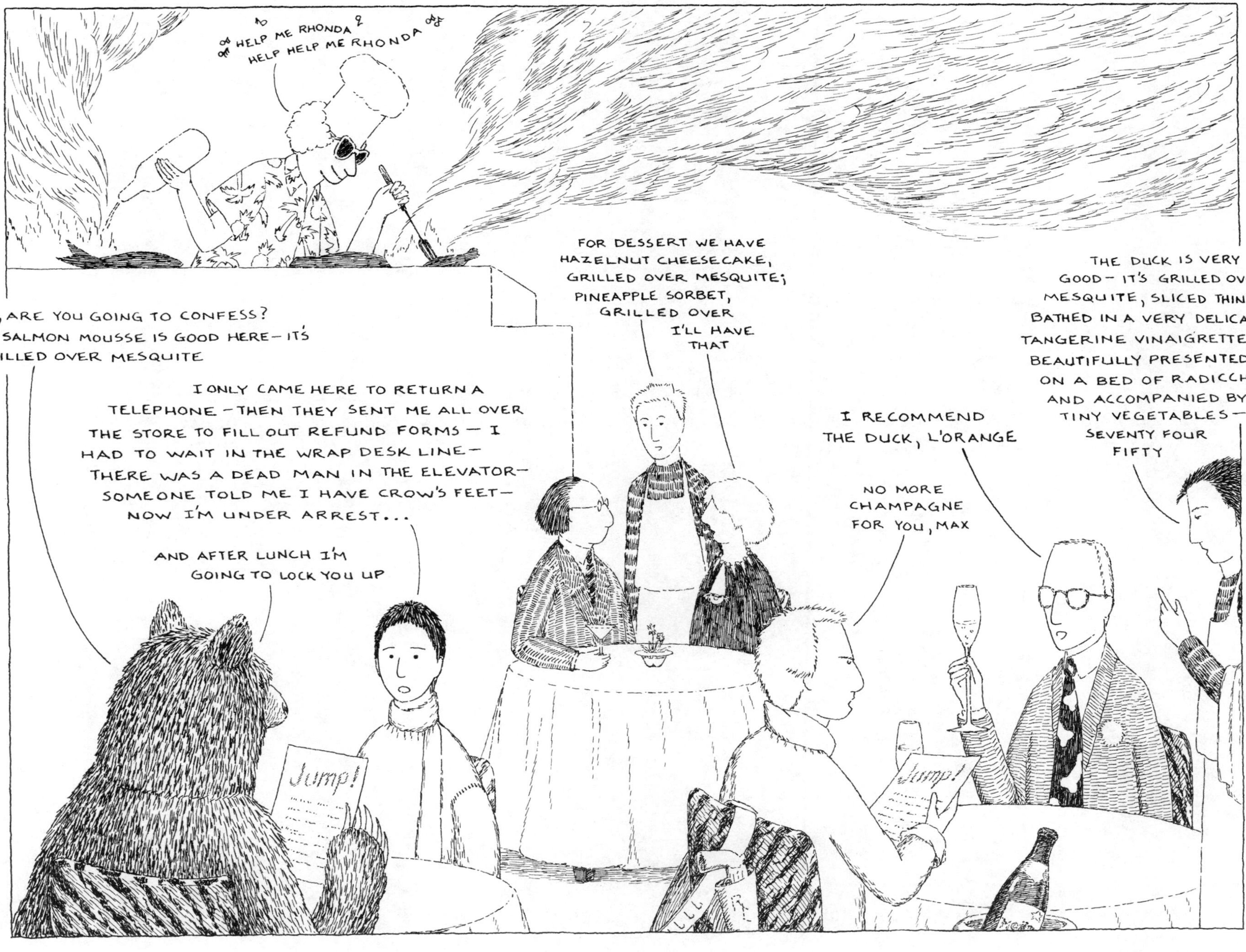
HELP ME RHONDA
HELP HELP ME RHONDA
SO, ARE YOU GOING TO CONFESS? THE SALMON MOUSSE IS GOOD HERE— IT'S GRILLED OVER MESQUITE
I ONLY CAME HERE TO RETURN A TELEPHONE—THEN THEY SENT ME ALL OVER THE STORE TO FILL OUT REFUND FORMS— I HAD TO WAIT IN THE WRAP DESK LINE— THERE WAS A DEAD MAN IN THE ELEVATOR— SOMEONE TOLD ME I HAVE CROW'S FEET— NOW I'M UNDER ARREST...
AND AFTER LUNCH I'M GOING TO LOCK YOU UP
FOR DESSERT WE HAVE HAZELNUT CHEESECAKE, GRILLED OVER MESQUITE; PINEAPPLE SORBET, GRILLED OVER
I'LL HAVE THAT
NO MORE CHAMPAGNE FOR YOU, MAX
I RECOMMEND THE DUCK, L'ORANGE
THE DUCK IS VERY GOOD— IT'S GRILLED OVER MESQUITE, SLICED THINLY, BATHED IN A VERY DELICATE TANGERINE VINAIGRETTE, BEAUTIFULLY PRESENTED ON A BED OF RADICCHIO AND ACCOMPANIED BY TINY VEGETABLES— SEVENTY FOUR FIFTY
Jump!
Jump!

RENFIELD HAD JUST FINISHED LUNCH. THE EMPLOYEES' CAFETERIA HAD A STRICT RULE AGAINST ZOOPHAGY, SO RENFIELD ALWAYS ATE LUNCH IN HIS OWN OFFICE, ALONE.

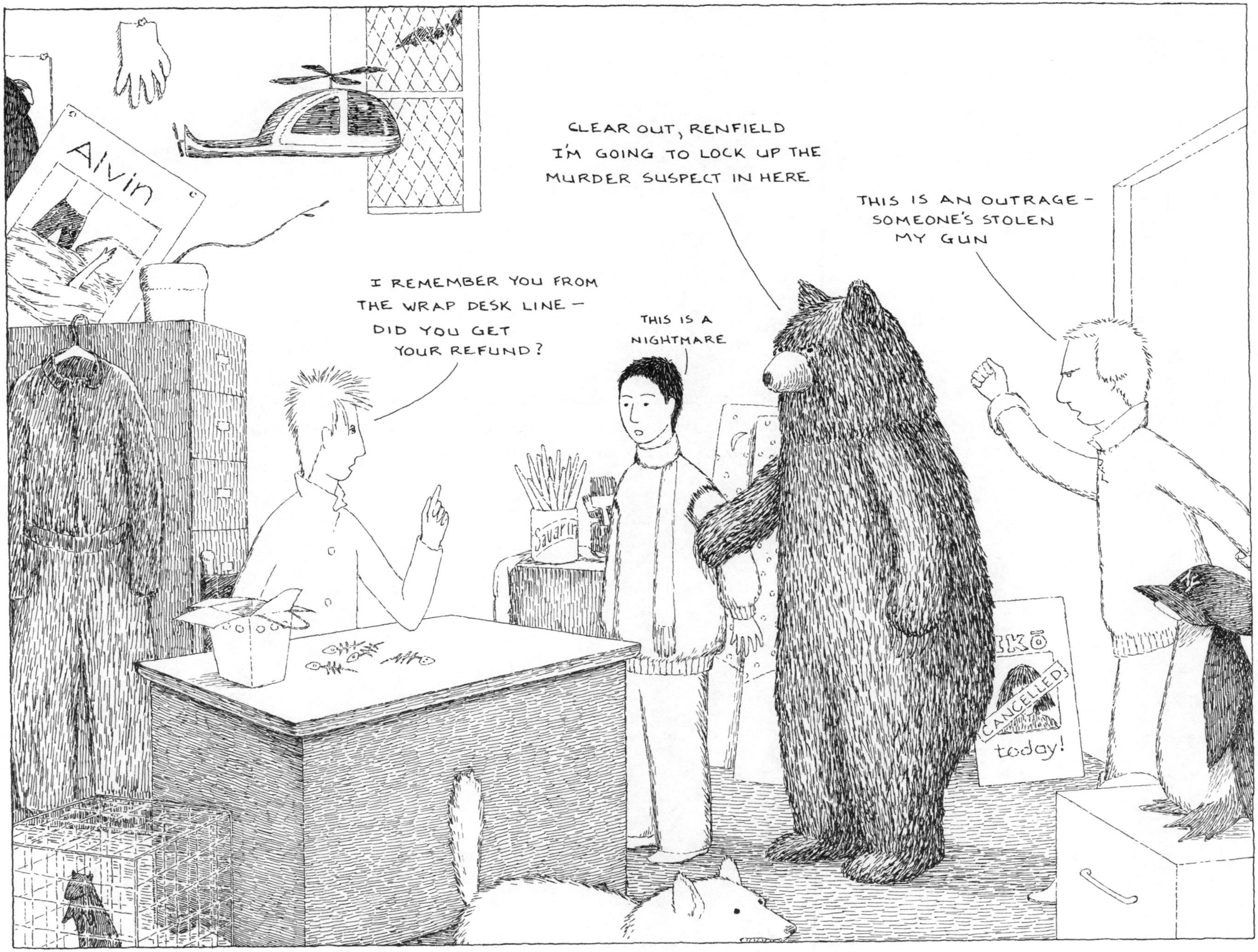

I REMEMBER YOU FROM THE WRAP DESK LINE — DID YOU GET YOUR REFUND?
THIS IS A NIGHTMARE
CLEAR OUT, RENFIELD I'M GOING TO LOCK UP THE MURDER SUSPECT IN HERE
THIS IS AN OUTRAGE — SOMEONE'S STOLEN MY GUN
Alvin
Savarin
CANCELLED
today!

Ikō was dead, and Rolf L'Orange was once again the most famous designer in the world, but he was not happy. Without his gun and holster, the outfit he was wearing was all wrong.

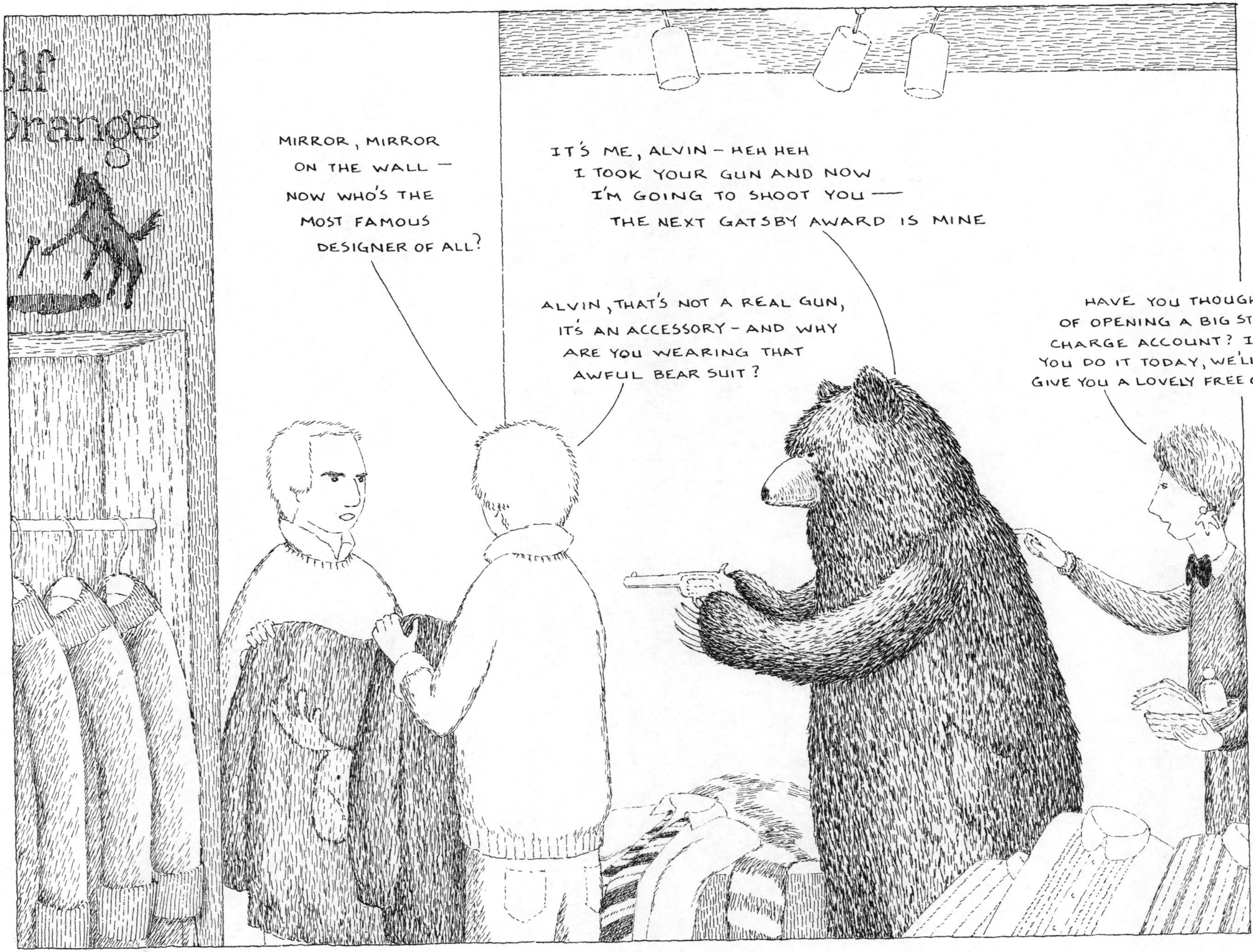
olf
Orange
MIRROR, MIRROR ON THE WALL — NOW WHO'S THE MOST FAMOUS DESIGNER OF ALL?
ALVIN, THAT'S NOT A REAL GUN, IT'S AN ACCESSORY — AND WHY ARE YOU WEARING THAT AWFUL BEAR SUIT?
IT'S ME, ALVIN — HEH HEH I TOOK YOUR GUN AND NOW I'M GOING TO SHOOT YOU — THE NEXT GATSBY AWARD IS MINE
HAVE YOU THOUGHT OF OPENING A BIG STORE CHARGE ACCOUNT? IF YOU DO IT TODAY, WE'LL GIVE YOU A LOVELY FREE GIFT

Discovering that the gun was useless, Alvin began to run. His mind had snapped.

STOP THAT BEAR — HE TRIED TO KILL ME HE'S INSANE
. . . AND IF YOU OPEN YOUR CHARGE ACCOUNT TODAY, WE'LL GIVE YOU A LOVELY FREE GIFT
THAT'S REDUNDANT- A GIFT IS FREE BY DEFINITION
QUEL HISTOIRE MÉCHANT
LOOK- ALL THESE IKŌ THINGS ARE HALF PRICE
DO I LOOK BETTER IN CLAMSHELL, OR DUST?
YOU'LL NEVER CATCH ME, ROLF — I KILLED IKŌ, AND I KILLED THE STORE DETECTIVE, TOO — I CAME HERE IN DISGUISE, BUT I FORGOT THIS STORE DOESN'T HAVE AN ELEVATOR MAN — THEN I SAW THE BEAR . . .

ALVIN RAN THROUGH THE BATH SHOP, HEADING FOR THE EXPRESS ELEVATOR. HE WAS OUT OF CONTROL.

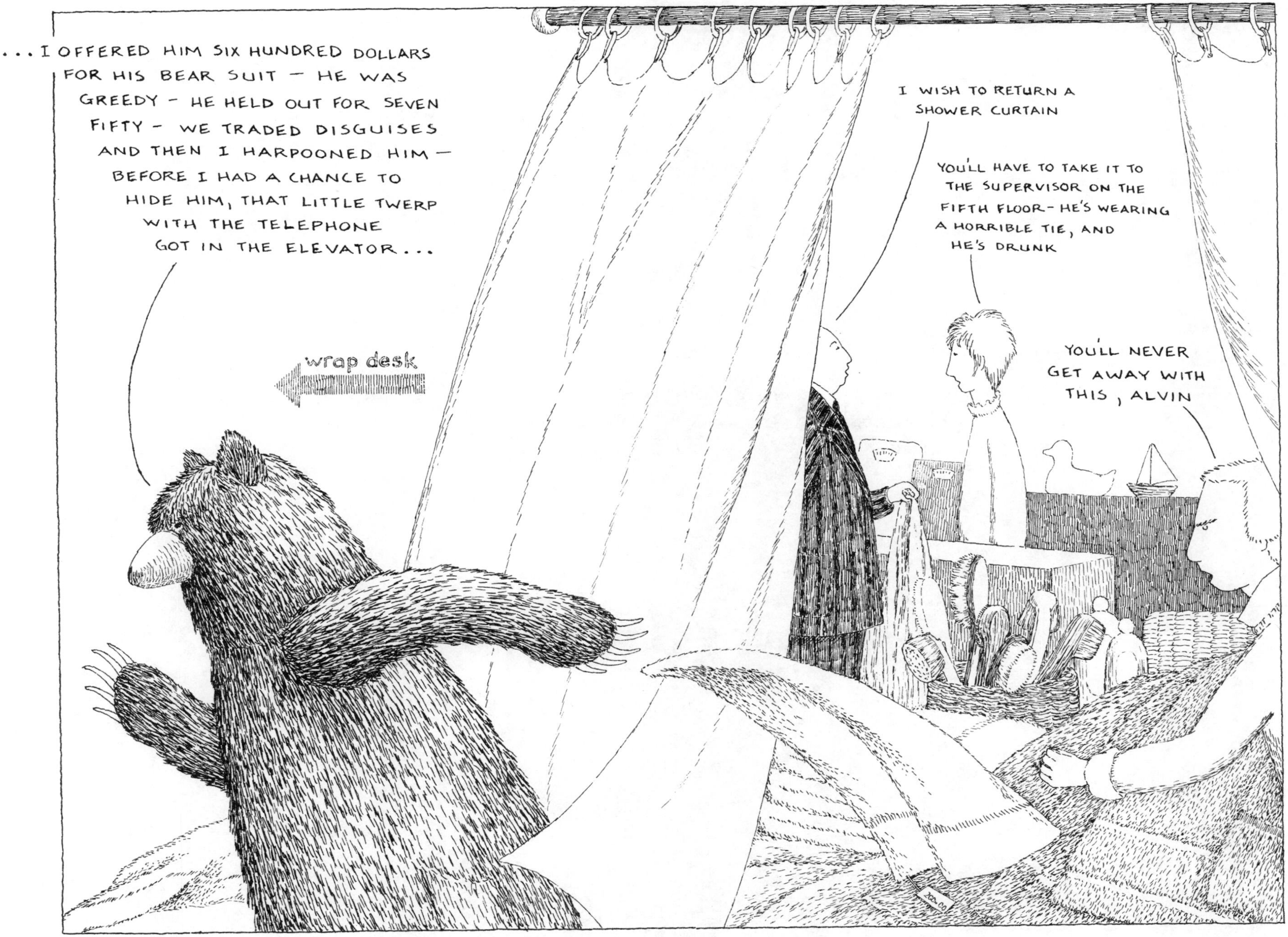
. . . I OFFERED HIM SIX HUNDRED DOLLARS FOR HIS BEAR SUIT – HE WAS GREEDY – HE HELD OUT FOR SEVEN FIFTY – WE TRADED DISGUISES AND THEN I HARPOONED HIM – BEFORE I HAD A CHANCE TO HIDE HIM, THAT LITTLE TWERP WITH THE TELEPHONE GOT IN THE ELEVATOR . . .
wrap desk
I WISH TO RETURN A SHOWER CURTAIN
YOU'LL HAVE TO TAKE IT TO THE SUPERVISOR ON THE FIFTH FLOOR – HE'S WEARING A HORRIBLE TIE, AND HE'S DRUNK
YOU'LL NEVER GET AWAY WITH THIS, ALVIN

THE WAY TO THE EXPRESS ELEVATOR WAS BLOCKED BY A WALL OF PEOPLE. ALVIN WAS DESPERATE. HE HAD TO GET TO THE OTHER SIDE OF THE WRAP DESK LINE.

WHAT'S HOLDING UP THE LINE? I CAN'T TAKE MUCH MORE OF THIS
THIS LINE HASN'T MOVED IN SIX HOURS— I'M STARVING
MY FEET HURT
THAT BEAR IS TRYING TO BREAK INTO THE LINE
... AND THEN THESE HALF HUMAN CREATURES FINALLY CAN'T TAKE ANY MORE OF RAYMOND BURR TREATING THEM LIKE ANIMALS, AND THEY START CLIMBING OUT OF THE PIT — BELA LUGOSI IS THEIR LEADER AND HE STARTS CHANTING "ARE WE NOT MEN?", AND THEN THEY GO AFTER RAYMOND BURR, ALL OF THEM SCREAMING...
ARE WE NOT MEN?
ARE WE NOT MEN?
I'LL DO IT— HEE HEE HEE HEE HEE
LOOK AT THAT BEAR— HE'S TRYING TO BREAK INTO THE LINE
HE'S NOT GETTING AHEAD OF ME
WHO DOES HE THINK HE IS?
STOP THAT BEAR

THEY TORE HIM TO PIECES.

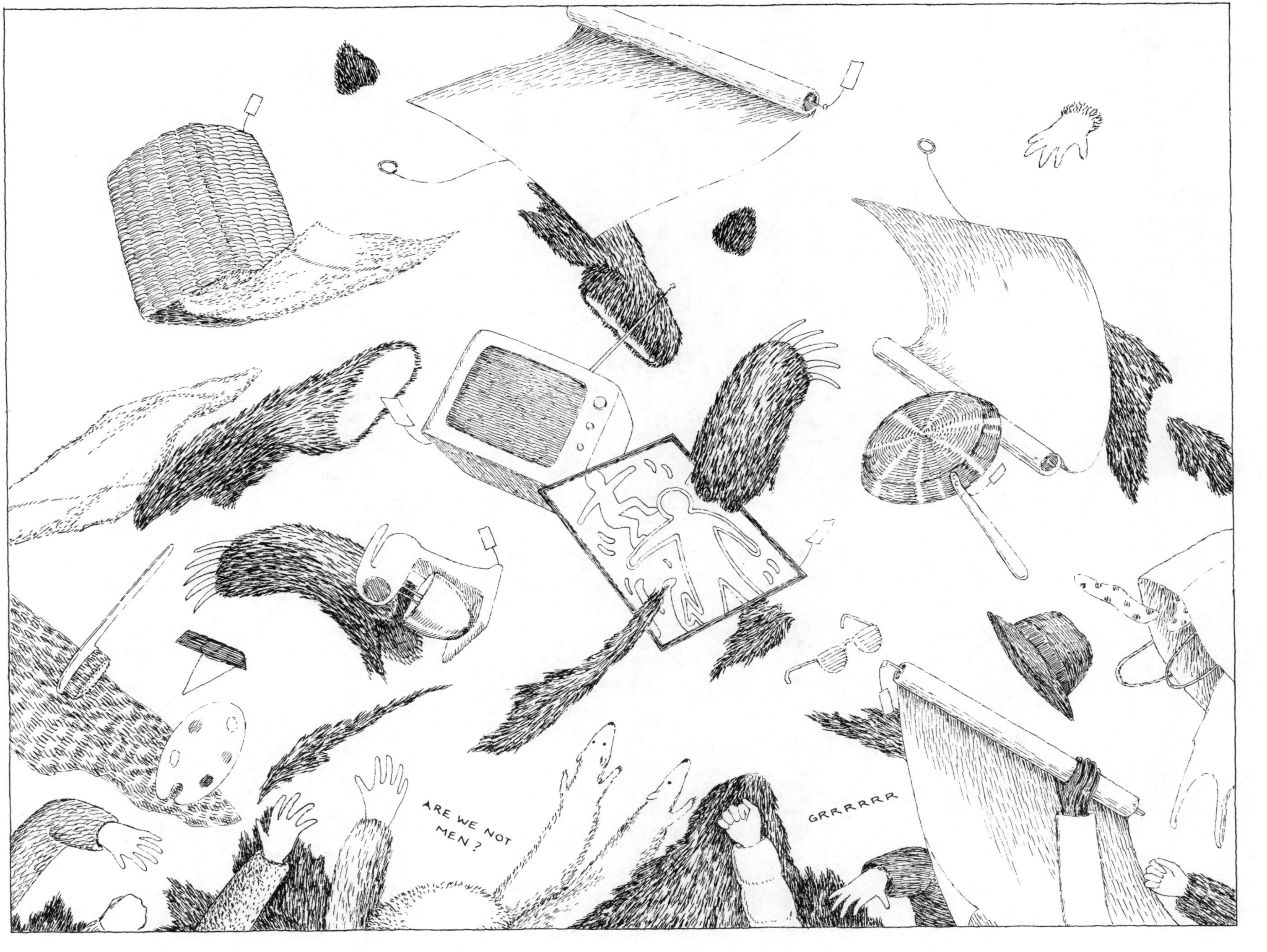
ARE WE NOT MEN?
GRRRRRR

EPILOGUE

NOTHING WAS LEFT OF ALVIN.

RENFIELD TOOK A VACATION. WHEN HE CAME BACK, IT WAS TIME FOR HIM TO CHANGE THE WINDOWS TO "SPRINGTIME IN SUMATRA", THE NEW THEME.

MAX WAS NEVER PROMOTED. IN HIS SPARE TIME HE WROTE A BOOK CALLED "DRESSING FOR FAILURE". IT BECAME A BEST SELLER AND MADE HIM RICH.

A. TUNA HAS AN IRRATIONAL FEAR OF DEPARTMENT STORES AND DOES ALL HER SHOPPING BY MAIL.

THE RADIO KILLER IS STILL AT LARGE.

ROLF L'ORANGE WON THE GATSBY AWARD.

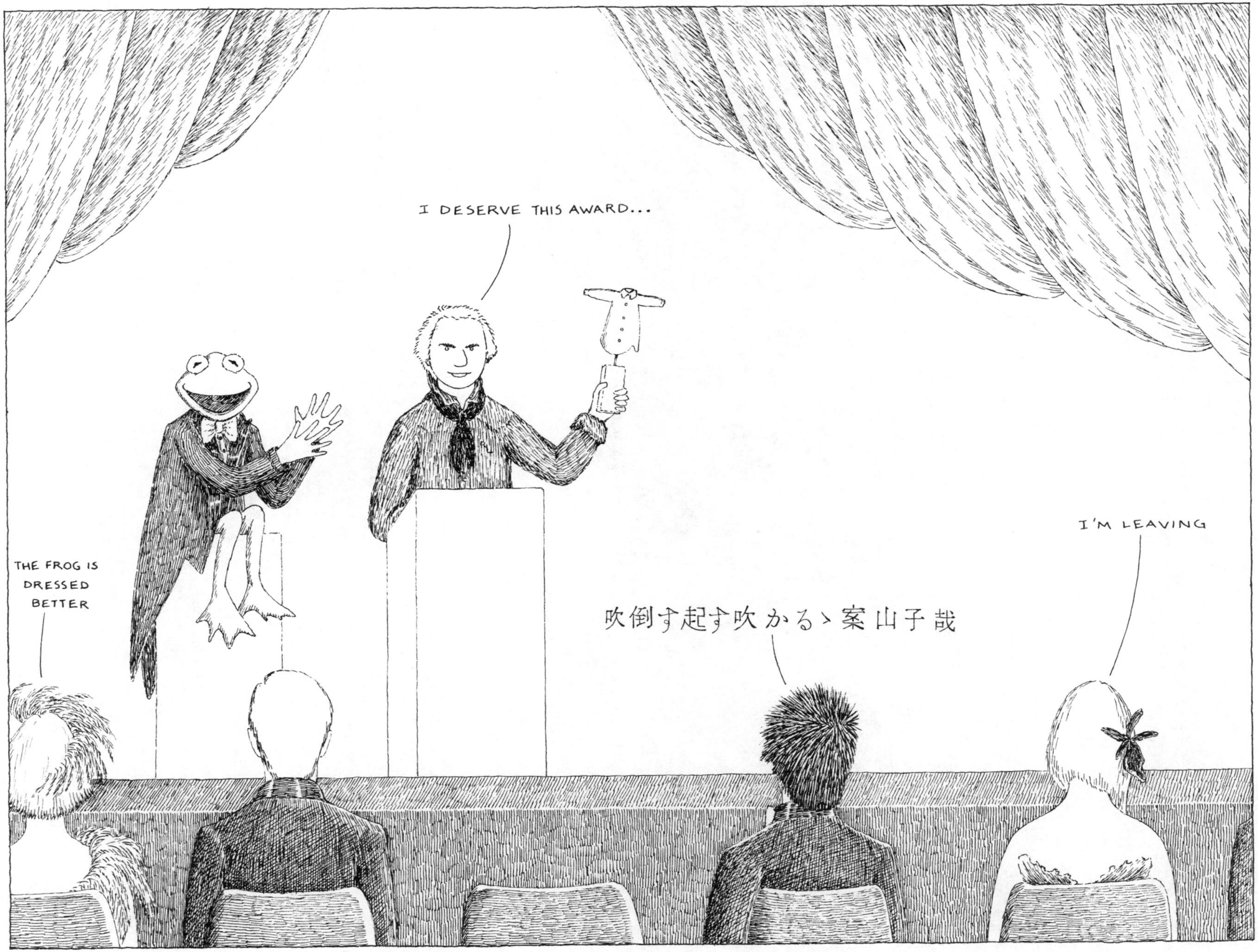
I DESERVE THIS AWARD...
THE FROG IS DRESSED BETTER
吹倒す起す吹かるゝ案山子哉
I'M LEAVING

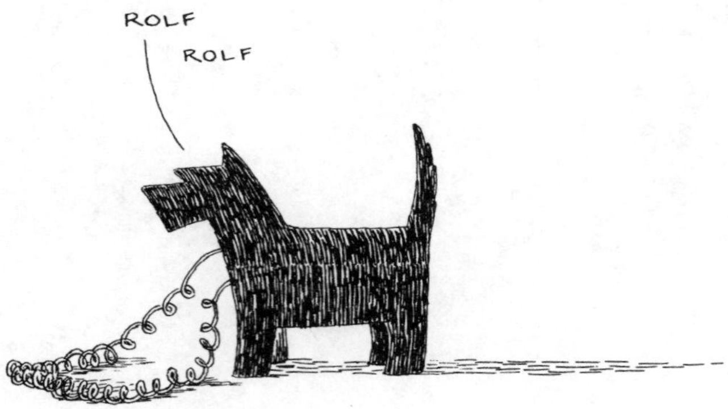
ROLF
ROLF